MINING IN AMERICA

# MINED PRODUCTS AND THEIR USES

BY CYNTHIA KENNEDY HENZEL

Cover image: Wulfenite crystal is a valuable mined product to gem collectors.

Core Library
An Imprint of Abdo Publishing
abdobooks.com

abdobooks.com

Published by Abdo Publishing, a division of ABDO, PO Box 398166, Minneapolis, Minnesota 55439. Copyright © 2024 by Abdo Consulting Group, Inc. International copyrights reserved in all countries. No part of this book may be reproduced in any form without written permission from the publisher. Core Library™ is a trademark and logo of Abdo Publishing.

Printed in the United States of America, North Mankato, Minnesota.
052023
092023

Cover Photo: Matteo Chinellato/Shutterstock Images
Interior Photos: Oleksandr Lysenko/Shutterstock Images, 4–5; Joe Buglewicz/Bloomberg/Getty Images, 7; Shutterstock Images, 9, 24, 43; Bernd Weissbrod/picture alliance/Getty Images, 11; Joey Ingelhart/E+/Getty Images, 12–13, 45; dszc/E+/Getty Images, 15; Red Line Editorial, 16; Orhan Cam/Shutterstock Images, 20–21; Chokniti Studio/Shutterstock Images, 22; Yulai Studio/Shutterstock Images, 28–29; Patrick T. Fallon/Bloomberg/Getty Images, 30; Ty Wright/Bloomberg/Getty Images, 34–35; Marcio Jose Sanchez/AP Images, 37

Editor: Angela Lim
Series Designer: Ryan Gale

**Library of Congress Control Number: 2022949135**

**Publisher's Cataloging-in-Publication Data**
Names: Henzel, Cynthia Kennedy, author.
Title: Mined products and their uses / by Cynthia Kennedy Henzel
Description: Minneapolis, Minnesota: Abdo Publishing Company, 2024 | Series: Mining in America | Includes online resources and index.
Identifiers: ISBN 9781098290948 (lib. bdg.) | ISBN 9781098277123 (ebook)
Subjects: LCSH: Mines and mining--Juvenile literature. | Mines and mineral resources--Juvenile literature. | Mining engineering--Juvenile literature. | United States--Juvenile literature.
Classification: DDC 622.0973--dc23

# CONTENTS

**CHAPTER ONE**
**What's in a Smartphone?** .......... 4

**CHAPTER TWO**
**Fossil Fuels** ..................... 12

**CHAPTER THREE**
**Rock and Clay** .................... 20

**CHAPTER FOUR**
**Gemstones** ....................... 28

**CHAPTER FIVE**
**Metals Change the World** ......... 34

Fast Facts ........................... 42

Stop and Think ....................... 44

Glossary ............................. 46

Online Resources ..................... 47

Learn More ........................... 47

Index ................................ 48

About the Author ..................... 48

Circuit board

# CHAPTER ONE

# WHAT'S IN A SMARTPHONE?

The bell rings, signaling the start of class. "Today we are going to study mined products," says Ms. Sams to her seventh-grade science class. She holds up a smartphone. "This product contains up to 62 types of metals. People mine metals."

Ms. Sams taps the phone's case. "This phone case is made of aluminum. Aluminum is a lightweight metal. It also bends easily. The aluminum in phone cases is mixed with magnesium or titanium to make it stronger.

**The circuit board of a phone holds the parts responsible for running programs on the device. It contains many mined materials.**

## TOUCH SCREENS

When a person uses a touch screen, a small electrical charge passes between the screen and the finger. The screen loses charge where it is touched. Sensors around the edges of the screen detect the change in charge and identify where the finger is touching. Glass does not conduct electricity well by itself, so the glass is coated with indium oxide combined with tin. Indium and tin are both mined materials. This coating makes the glass very conductive.

Aluminum, magnesium, and titanium are mined metals."

She turns the phone over. "Phones include other mined materials. The glass screen is made of silicon, aluminum, and potassium."

Ms. Sams explains that phones contain up to 16 rare earth metals. "Rare earth metals are not uncommon underground. But they are difficult to mine because they are often found in ores, which contain a mixture of minerals. It is difficult to separate the metal from the ore." She pulls up an image of a rainbow on the phone. "Rare earth metals create the colors we see onscreen."

**Mountain Pass mine in California is a major producer of ores containing rare earth metals.**

The teacher opens the phone and points to its battery. "This is a lithium battery. Lithium is a mined metal that can hold an electrical charge for a long time. Big lithium batteries power electric cars."

She indicates a flat area inside the phone covered with tiny boxes. "This is the circuit board. It is made out of plastic. Plastic is a product that comes from petroleum, another mined material. Phones work by receiving and sending out radio signals. One reason circuit boards use plastic is because radio signals pass through plastic more easily than through metal.

## PERSPECTIVES
### RECYCLING SMARTPHONES

Smartphones are made from mined materials that can cause pollution if not disposed of properly. Recycling smartphones is also important because mining new materials for products is bad for the environment. David Cole-Hamilton has researched smartphones and their effect on the planet. He suggested ways for people to limit this impact. He said, "People should keep their phones for longer, . . . give the phone to someone else if they have to get a new one, . . . and hand [them] in to a company that does ethical recycling once they really cannot be used anymore."

Copper, gold, nickel, and zinc are among the other mined materials used on the circuit board."

She continues, "But what really makes the smartphone work are silicon computer chips. Silica sand is mined and mixed with carbon. The mixture is then heated to high temperatures to extract silicon. The material is cut into very thin slices to form chips to hold transistors. A transistor is a tiny device that controls the flow of

# MINED MATERIALS IN A SMARTPHONE

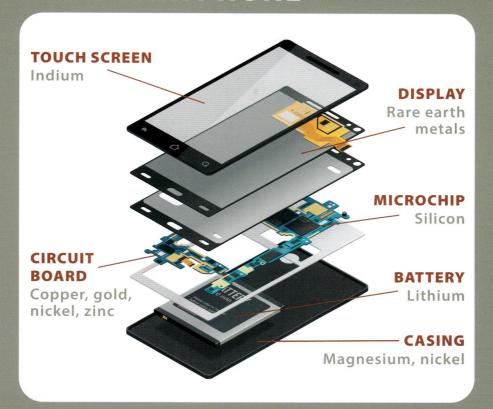

Many mined materials are used to make a smartphone. Was the number of materials needed to make a phone surprising? How do you think mining and the future of electronics are connected?

electricity in electronic equipment. Silicon chips make all modern electronics possible."

"Wow," says Carl. "My phone runs on sand."

Ms. Sams laughs. "Yes, as well as dozens of other mined products from around the world."

## FROM THE GROUND

Many products people use every day come from mined materials. Mined products, such as iron for steel beams and copper for wiring, are used to build homes. Some clothes are made of petroleum products such as polyester, nylon, and spandex. Mined materials supply power to run vehicles. They are in fertilizers used to grow food.

Some mined products, such as gravel, are not processed, or changed from their original form, before use. Other mined materials, such as petroleum, must be processed before they can be used. Chemists and engineers create new products by combining materials in new ways. Mined products are essential in today's world.

**Many construction materials, including steel and concrete, are made from mined substances.**

CHAPTER
TWO

# FOSSIL FUELS

Fossil fuels are mined materials that come from decaying plants and animals. Coal, oil, and natural gas are fossil fuels. People can burn these fuels for energy to heat homes, cook, power vehicles, and produce electricity.

In 2021, the United States mined approximately 577 million tons (523 million metric tons) of coal. It was the most mined material in the country. About 23 percent of US electricity is produced from burning coal.

**Burning coal is a major source of electricity in the United States. But doing so releases gases that contribute to climate change.**

## PERSPECTIVES
### WORKING IN A COAL MINE

Curtis Burton is a coal miner. He explains that it can take several hours of traveling through tunnels to get to the coal. It is dark. The air pressure underground can cause ears to pop. Ceilings are bolted for safety, but collapses still happen. Sometimes toxic gases such as carbon monoxide and methane are released during mining. If methane mixes with coal dust, it can cause an explosion. Burton says that although mining is dangerous, it pays well and is a unique job: "Every day when you go underground you're seeing a part of the earth nobody else is seeing ever. I always thought it was neat."

Four different types of coal are mined in the United States. Each type has a different amount of carbon and is used for different purposes. Coal that has a higher amount of carbon can produce more heat.

Bituminous coal is the most common type of coal in the United States. It produces a lot of heat when burned. It is also used to generate electricity. Bituminous coal is also used to make coke, the fuel used

**Texas produces the most crude oil of any US state.**

to produce steel. The process of creating coke creates dark, gooey tar. This tar is used in products that treat dandruff and head lice.

## PETROLEUM

Petroleum, or crude oil, is usually blackish in color. It is pumped as a liquid from deep underground. Petroleum is a mixture of chemicals that vary by fluidity. Some parts of petroleum flow like water. Other parts may be thick and sticky. Heavy forms of petroleum are solid at room temperature.

# PETROLEUM PRODUCTS MADE FROM REFINED OIL

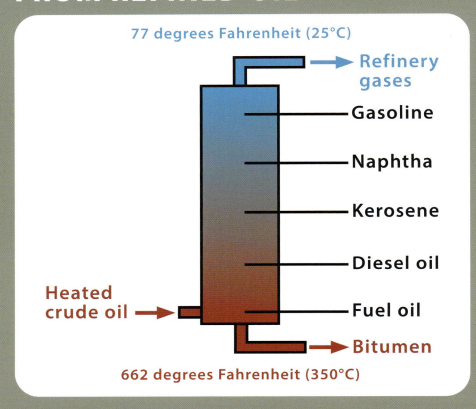

In an oil refinery, petroleum is heated to separate the oil into different products. Some parts of the petroleum become gas at lower temperatures than other parts. How does this help you understand why petroleum can be used to make so many products?

Petroleum needs to be refined, or processed, before it can be made into useful products such as gasoline. Gasoline is made from a fluid, lightweight petroleum. It produces an explosion when ignited. This energy can be used to power engines. More than half the petroleum used in the United States serves as fuel for transportation.

Thicker crude oils do not vaporize at normal temperatures. This makes them useful for lubricants that grease machinery. Vaseline is also made from less-fluid petroleum. Bitumen oil is thick and sticky. It is used to make asphalt for roads. Paraffin wax is an example of a heavy petroleum. It melts only when heated at extremely high temperatures.

Petroleum is also used to make naphtha. This clear liquid vaporizes quickly.

## NATURAL GAS

Natural gas is colorless and odorless. It is a fossil fuel that is formed deep underground. Natural gas is composed primarily of methane. Sometimes the gas is found in pockets near oil deposits. Natural gas is very flammable. It is often used to heat buildings. Because people cannot breathe natural gas, producers give it a smell before it is sold. This makes it easier to detect gas leaks.

It is used in paint solvents and quick-drying products. Naphtha is the essential material used to make plastics. Though less than 10 percent of petroleum is used to make plastic, many everyday products are made from this material. Plastic can be found in food containers, clothing, electronics, and other household items.

When petroleum products are burned, they produce carbon dioxide. Carbon dioxide is then trapped in the atmosphere. This gas holds on to heat and influences climate change. Plastics made from petroleum can take thousands of years to break down. Plastic waste is harmful to wildlife.

The United States is the largest consumer of petroleum in the world. People living in the United States make up only around 4 percent of the world's population. But the country uses more than 20 percent of the petroleum produced worldwide. The United States is also the world's largest oil producer. The country produces approximately 20 percent of all petroleum.

# STRAIGHT TO THE
# SOURCE

Microplastics, or tiny plastic particles, are a major pollutant. Marine scientist Imogen Napper explains her research on microplastics in the marine environment:

> *When I think of plastic, I automatically think of a plastic bag or a water bottle, but for me the small bits (microplastics) are the most problematic. A plastic bag could break down into thousands of tiny bits, and how do we effectively remove that from the ocean? . . . There are so many small steps we can do to be more environmental, such as buying second-hand clothes and minimizing how much single-use plastic we take. All little steps help.*
>
> Source: Margaux Monfared. "Investigating Plastic Pollution." *Women in Ocean Science*, 2 July 2020, womeninoceanscience.com. Accessed 15 Dec. 2022.

## BACK IT UP

The author of this passage is using evidence to support a point. Write a paragraph describing the point the author is making. Then write down two or three pieces of evidence the author uses to make the point.

# CHAPTER THREE

# ROCK AND CLAY

Rocks are mined to create many products. Some rocks do not need to be processed before they are used. For example, sand is used as it naturally occurs in the ground. This material is comfortable to walk on and drains water well. It is spread on human-made beaches and playgrounds. Gravel covers roads or walking paths to make them less muddy. It also prevents dust from becoming airborne. Sand and gravel can also be mixed with

**The white marble used in the Washington Monument in Washington, DC, came from three different quarries in the United States.**

*Some types of clay can be used to make pottery.*

cement to make concrete for roads, sidewalks, bridges, and buildings.

Clay is made of very small particles of rock. It is sticky and malleable when it is wet. Clay requires little processing. It is mixed with sand before it can be used. Clay can be formed into different shapes and then dried. Bricks can be made from this material.

Clays come in different colors. Some types need to be heated at higher temperatures to harden. Some clays are easier to shape than others. Clay is also porous. This means the material has small holes that allow air and water to pass through. This material is often used for flowerpots because it allows plants to breathe. Porcelain clay is the least flexible. It is used to create sturdy objects, such as fine dinnerware.

## ROCKS IN CONSTRUCTION

Limestone is one of the most important rocks used in construction. It is a sedimentary rock that takes many forms. Dense limestone is strong and not very porous.

Limestone can be cut into blocks. It can also be sliced into thin tiles. Under high pressure, limestone becomes marble. This is a hard stone used to make countertops and statues. Processed limestone has other uses. It can be used for road bases and building foundations. Limestone is mixed with crushed shale at high temperatures to make cement.

The United States is the largest producer of gypsum in the world. It mined more than 25 million tons (23 million metric tons) in 2021.

Chalk is a soft form of limestone. It can be crushed into a fine power called whiting. Whiting is used to make putty, pigment in paints, glazes for pottery, plastics, paper, and other items.

Gypsum is a soft, white rock. It is the main ingredient in plaster of Paris, which is used to make casts for broken bones. In construction, gypsum is used to create drywall panels. Alabaster is a variety of gypsum. It is used for sculptures and pottery.

Asbestos is a mined mineral made of thin, flexible fibers. It is resistant to heat, electricity, and corrosion.

Asbestos was once commonly used in insulation, paint, flooring, and other construction materials. But research showed that breathing asbestos fibers causes lung disease and cancer, so mining for asbestos is banned in the United States. However, many older buildings still contain asbestos.

## ROCKS AND AGRICULTURE

Some mined products can be added to soil to help plants grow.

# PERSPECTIVES
## SALT MINING

Much of the salt mined in the United States is spread on roads in the winter to melt snow. Miners who work in the American Rock Salt mine in western New York are busy when there is bad weather. Heavy snow means a higher demand for salt. Miners, such as John Goho, descend 1,200 feet (366 m) underground into a system of long tunnels. They use explosives to loosen salt. Then they scoop the loose salt into a rock-crushing machine and send it to the surface. Goho says he has always considered coming into the mine like going to a health spa because the airborne salt seems to help his sinuses.

Potash is a mined salt that is rich in the nutrient potassium. Potassium is essential for plant growth. Ninety-five percent of the potash mined in the world is used in farming. Potash is also used in detergents and soaps to remove stains. It is used in medicines and explosives too.

Gypsum can be added to the soil to provide calcium and sulfur. It improves soil quality. It changes the structure of the soil so that water moves more freely. Gypsum can also be added directly to food as a source

> ### FIRST PATENT IN THE UNITED STATES
> Ash from burnt hardwood trees was an early source of potash. The first patent issued in the United States was for a process and machine to make potash. It was signed by George Washington on July 31, 1790, and issued to Samuel Hopkins. Hopkins used a furnace to reburn ashes. This improved the purity of the potash. In the early 1800s, the United States was the world's main producer of potash. But in the 1860s, German chemists discovered how to mine potash. People no longer got this mineral from ash.

of calcium. It is put in foods such as canned vegetables and ice cream.

Finely crushed limestone is spread on agricultural fields. It reduces acid in the soil. Crushed limestone is a source of calcium. It is fed to chickens to help them produce eggs with strong shells.

Salt is a mined product that is rich in sodium. The human body requires sodium for nerve and muscle health. Salt is also used to preserve foods such as meat, fish, and cabbage. This is because bacteria cannot live in high amounts of salt.

## FURTHER EVIDENCE

Chapter Three talks about how rocks are used in everyday life. What was one of the main points of this chapter? What evidence is included to support this point? Read the article at the website below. Does the information on the website support the main point of the chapter? Does it present new evidence?

### ROCKS AND MINERALS: EVERYDAY USES
abdocorelibrary.com/mined-products

## CHAPTER FOUR

# GEMSTONES

**G**emstones are minerals that are known for their value and beauty. Diamonds, rubies, and emeralds are examples of gemstones. Mining companies and governments have a history of forcing people to mine diamonds. Some people have mined diamonds during wars, selling them to make money to purchase weapons. These are called blood diamonds, and it is illegal to purchase them. Today, diamonds can be

**Some saw blades that can cut through stone are partially made from diamonds.**

**Diamonds that are used for jewelry are carefully inspected for clarity and lack of flaws.**

manufactured in laboratories. But diamonds are still mined for their value and rarity.

Approximately 80 percent of mined diamonds are used for products other than jewelry. Diamonds are the hardest naturally occurring material on Earth. Particles of diamond are used on sawblades, allowing these tools to cut metal and stone. These gemstones are also used in medicine because they resist bacteria. They can be ground into tiny particles called nanodiamonds, which can deliver vaccines or drugs into the body. Diamonds may one day be used to build bionic eyes.

Diamonds conduct heat well. They can be used to keep electronic devices cool. Other gemstones are also used in machinery and electronics. A wide range of light can pass through sapphires. These gemstones are used in fingerprint authentication sensors and barcode readers at cash registers. Rubies are used in red lasers, which are powerful enough to cut holes in diamonds.

## QUARTZ

Quartz is a mineral made of silicon and oxygen. Quartz can be ground into sand called silica. It is used to make concrete, glass, and ceramics.

Quartz crystals have properties that make them useful for electronics.

## SPINTRONICS

Diamonds may be at the cutting edge of a new age of electronics called spintronics. Silicon chips use electrical charges to store data. But the amount of data that can be stored on a chip is limited. Spintronics uses the spin of a material's electrons, rather than just their electrical charge, to store and transfer data. Spintronics works with other semiconductors. But it is easier for scientists to control the spin of electrons in diamonds than in other materials. This new technology would allow greater data storage than silicon chips.

# PERSPECTIVES

## FRACKING

**Silica is used in fracking. This is the process of using pressurized water, sand, and chemicals to break apart rock deep underground. Fracking is used to access natural gas and petroleum. The water used in fracking can pollute nearby water sources. Fracking can also increase the risk of earthquakes. An earthquake was recorded in western Texas in November 2022. Some residents, including David Shifflett, believed fracking was the cause. He said, "[The Texas government] is . . . letting [oil companies] put too much high pressure under the ground too close to the surface."**

The material is conductive. When an electrical current passes through quartz, it causes the crystal to vibrate exactly 32,768 times a second. This vibration is used to keep time in electronics such as watches and computers. A circuit connected to the quartz counts the number of vibrations. It calculates how much time has passed.

Silicon is the second most abundant element in the Earth's crust, but it does not occur alone in nature. It can be separated from silica using heat.

Silicon is a semiconductive material. This means that it is not as conductive as metals, but it still allows an electrical current to pass through it. The conductivity can be altered by adding other materials to the silicon. Silicon chips make modern electronics possible.

Silicon is also the primary material used to make silicone. Silicone is a rubbery material that is resistant to both temperature and water. These qualities make silicone caulk an effective product to fill cracks around windows or bathtubs. Silicone is also used to make products including cookware and electrical insulators.

## EXPLORE ONLINE

Chapter Four talks about the importance of diamonds in industry. Today diamonds of equal quality to mined diamonds can be manufactured in laboratories. Read the following website and think about whether you would support using only lab diamonds in industry.

### IS GROWING DIAMONDS A SUSTAINABLE ALTERNATIVE TO DIAMOND MINING?

abdocorelibrary.com/mined-products

## CHAPTER FIVE

# METALS CHANGE THE WORLD

Metals are elements that conduct electricity and heat. They are usually solid, reflective, and able to be pressed or hammered into various shapes. Many metals, including copper, can be stretched into thin wires.

Iron is the most mined metal on Earth. It is heavy and inexpensive, and it has a high melting point. Iron is used for construction beams, bike chains, and tools. It is also used to make cast-iron cookware. Iron is a porous

**Iron melts at 2,750 degrees Fahrenheit (1,510°C). The melted metal can be poured into molds and shaped.**

material that allows cooking oil and fats to bond to the cookware and create a nonstick surface.

Copper is a malleable metal that conducts electricity very easily. It is used in electrical wiring. Copper kills bacteria and viruses. This makes it good for cookware, water pipes, and handrails. As copper reacts to oxygen, it forms a green coating that makes it resistant to breaking down. This makes it useful construction material for rooftops. Statues such as the Statue of Liberty are made from copper.

Aluminum is an element that is commonly found in a mineral called bauxite. The metal can be easily shaped to make products such as soda cans and aluminum foil. Airplanes and space vehicles are built with aluminum because it is lightweight but strong. Power lines are made from aluminum. The lighter weight makes it easier to stretch electric wires between poles.

Lithium is the most lightweight metal. It is mined from the ground or from evaporating water from some salty lakes. Lithium is used in some medicines that treat

Geothermal plants stand near California's Salton Sea. In 2022, companies began to explore the region as a source of lithium.

mood disorders. Lithium also has a high capacity to store energy. This makes lithium a great material for making rechargeable batteries to power electric cars. Demand for this metal is increasing with the demand for electric vehicles.

## METAL ALLOYS

A metal alloy is a mixture of a metal and another element. Alloys can increase the strength or performance of a metal. Steel is an alloy of iron and carbon. It is stronger than iron and resists rusting, so steel is often preferred over iron for construction.

Stainless steel, an alloy of steel and chromium, is not as strong as steel. It has a shiny surface that will not stain, so it is often used for appliances or cookware.

Brass is an alloy of copper and zinc. It has a yellow color that makes it popular for decorations such as cabinet knobs. Many musical instruments are made of brass because the metal is easy to bend and form but is very durable.

Copper alloyed with tin makes bronze. Bronze is harder than pure copper. Bronze is used in bells, guitar strings, and sculptures.

## PRECIOUS METALS

Precious metals are metals that are rare and valuable. Gold, silver, and platinum are precious metals. Of all metals, silver is the best conductor of electricity and heat. It is malleable and can be flattened into thin sheets or wires. It is commonly used for electronics in automobiles, such as the lines that melt ice on windows. Silver can also be made into paste. In this form, silver helps capture and transform the sun's rays into electricity in solar panels.

Silver is important in medicine. When exposed to light, silver crystals record X-ray images. Silver kills bacteria, so it is an ingredient in some antibiotic medicines.

Today, approximately 78 percent of mined gold is used for jewelry. Gold is highly conductive and does not corrode easily. This makes the metal useful in other products. Gold is used to make thin wires and tiny switches in electronics. Gold is also used for dental work such as fillings. It has medicinal properties. People are not allergic to gold. The metal is used in some treatments for cancer and other diseases.

## GOLD IN SPACE

The National Aeronautics and Space Administration is the US space program. It uses gold on the insides of space vehicles because it shields against radiation. Gold reflects infrared light, but it lets in visible light. The visors astronauts wear have a layer of gold that protects their eyes from the sun.

# PERSPECTIVES

## LEAD

Lead is a soft, malleable metal. It was once used in many products, including paint. Scientists learned that even small amounts of lead caused problems with the brain and nervous system. Lead paint was banned in 1978. But it is still found in older homes. Michigan state officials have taken steps to help ensure that children can receive treatment for lead poisoning. Diane McCloskey is the executive director of a nonprofit group focused on limiting lead poisoning in children. She said, "The quicker we can stop [children] from being exposed and the more we can educate parents, the better it's going to be for the child."

Mined products are everywhere and affect every part of people's lives. Scientists are constantly creating new products from mined materials, such as food additives and medical devices. Mined materials help with agriculture. Products such as gasoline and lithium batteries are used in transportation. Many industries and technologies require mined materials.

# STRAIGHT TO THE
# SOURCE

Environmental activists believe the development of Rhyolite Ridge Mine, a lithium mine, will threaten Tiehm's buckwheat. This is an endangered wildflower species that grows on nearby land. Patrick Donnelly is the Great Basin director at the Center for Biological Diversity. In 2022 he spoke about the mine and endangered species:

> *Rhyolite Ridge Mine poses an existential threat to Tiehm's buckwheat, and we're gearing up for a fight. . . . We have to transition to renewable energy to address the climate emergency, but we can't wipe plants and animals off the planet in the process. If the Biden administration wants the renewable energy transition to succeed, it needs to devise a plan that doesn't drive species extinct.*
>
> Source: "BLM Starts Permitting for Nevada Lithium Mine That Threatens Rare Wildflower." *Center for Biological Diversity*, 19 Dec. 2022, biologicaldiversity.org. Accessed 19 Dec. 2022.

## WHAT'S THE BIG IDEA?

Take a close look at this passage. What is the main connection between the demand for lithium and endangered species? Why can it be difficult to prepare for a future using renewable energy?

# FAST FACTS

- Petroleum, coal, and natural gas are fuels that can be used for heating, transportation, and generating electricity.

- Petroleum is used to make plastics and other everyday products.

- Potash and potassium are important fertilizers for crops.

- Diamonds are the hardest natural material on Earth. They are used in cutting tools, electronics, and medicine.

- Quartz is an important construction material. Silicon can be separated from quartz sand. This material is vital for creating silicon chips that power computers.

- Iron is hard and sturdy. It is used to make steel. Iron and steel are used for constructing buildings, building railroad tracks, and manufacturing engines.

- Copper conducts electricity well and is used in wiring and electronics.

- Aluminum is lightweight and strong, so it is used in aircraft.

- Lithium is lightweight and holds an electrical charge. It is essential for the rechargeable batteries used in electric cars today.

- Gold and silver are good conductors and are often used in electronics. They are also used in medicines.

# STOP AND THINK

### Another View

Fossil fuels are essential to the way of life today, but using them leads to climate change. As you know, every source is different. Ask an adult to help you find another source about this fact. Write a short essay comparing and contrasting the new source's point of view with that of this book's author. What is the point of view of each author? How are they similar and why? How are they different and why?

### You Are There

This book discusses materials such as coal and diamonds that are mined from deep underground. Imagine you work in an underground mine. Discuss how you might spend your day. What does the mine look like?

### Surprise Me

Chapter Four discusses uses of gems in industry. After reading the chapter, what two or three facts about gems did you find most surprising and why? Write a few sentences about each fact.

## Dig Deeper

After reading this book, what questions do you still have about mined products and their uses? With an adult's help, find a few reliable sources that can help you answer your questions. Write a paragraph about what you have learned.

# GLOSSARY

**circuit**
the path by which electricity travels in a device

**conductive**
able to transmit electricity

**corrosion**
the process of wearing away and breaking down

**electron**
a negatively charged particle

**flammable**
easily ignited and burned

**lubricant**
a substance used between moving parts so they are able to move over each other easily

**malleable**
able to be shaped without breaking or cracking

**patent**
a government license giving the sole right for a company or individual to build and sell an invention for a period of time

**sedimentary rock**
a type of rock that is made from the collection of other materials, usually brought together by water

**vaporize**
to become a vapor or gas

# ONLINE RESOURCES

To learn more about mined products and their uses, visit our free resource websites below.

Visit **abdocorelibrary.com** or scan this QR code for free Common Core resources for teachers and students, including vetted activities, multimedia, and booklinks, for deeper subject comprehension.

Visit **abdobooklinks.com** or scan this QR code for free additional online weblinks for further learning. These links are routinely monitored and updated to provide the most current information available.

# LEARN MORE

Gagne, Tammy. *Mineral Processing*. Abdo, 2024.

Lusted, Marcia Amidon. *Fossils, Rocks, and Minerals*. Abdo, 2022.

Newland, Sonya. *Working with Materials*. Kane Miller, 2020.

# INDEX

alloys, 37–38
aluminum, 5–6, 36

batteries, 7, 9, 37, 40

coal, 13–14
construction, 10, 22–25, 35–37
copper, 8, 9, 10 35–36, 38

electricity, 6–7, 9, 13–14, 24, 31, 32–33, 35–39
electronics, 9, 18, 30–33, 38–39

gasoline, 16–17, 40
gold, 8, 9, 38–39
gravel, 10, 21
gypsum, 24, 26–27

iron, 10, 35–37

limestone, 23–24, 27
lithium, 7, 9, 36–37, 40, 41

medicine, 26, 30, 36–37, 39–40

natural gas, 13, 17, 32

petroleum, 7, 10, 15–18, 32
plastics, 7, 18, 19, 24

quartz, 31–32

rare earth metals, 6, 9

sand, 8–9, 21–22, 31, 32
silicon, 6, 8–9, 31–33
silver, 38–39

vehicles, 10, 13, 36–37, 39

## About the Author

Cynthia Kennedy Henzel has a BS in social studies education and an MS in geography. She has worked as a teacher in many countries. Currently, she writes fiction and nonfiction books and develops education materials for social studies, history, science, and ELL students. She has written more than 100 books and over 150 stories for young people.